WHAT PROFESSIONALS ARE SAYING ABOUT "SUDDENLY SINGLE!"

W9-CEK-500

"The book has a gentle rhythm that flows through the grief process, respecting the uniqueness of every person. It's easy reading; it offers something for all personalities, the intuitive creator as well as the organized thinker. I enjoyed it tremendously."

> *Jane A. Bouma – Saldana*
> *Marital and Family Therapist*
> *Professor, International University*

"I am greatly impressed with the book's simplicity and clarity in conveying such difficult psychological experiences relating to the loss of loved ones, together with the uncanny ability to explain to the reader the complex psychodynamics of loss with accuracy and illuminating insight — all in such a simple and impressively poetic style."

> *Dean Salama, M.D., M.C.R.P.*
> *Psychiatrist, Retired*
> *Ridgewood, New Jersey*

"Absolutely wonderful material...does not insult the reader's intelligence...provides hope and a sense of direction...contains readily applicable ideas. I definitely will recommend the book to many of my own patients and friends."

> *John A. Buehler, M.D., Ph.D.*
> *Psychiatrist*
> *Kentfield, CA*

[i]

"I love the book. It is about time somebody cut through the jungle of information about loss, separation and grief, and made something practical, useful and inspiring as this."

> Mariano Barragan, M.D.
> Psychiatrist
> Founder, Mexican Institute of
> Psychotherapy

"It is comforting, supportive and most helpful to those who find themselves again single...emotional, intellectual and poetic support...balm to a wide variety of emotional types. The ideas presented can contribute to the growth of a personal philosophy that can provide succor to the weakest, and broad nourishment to the strongest so both can go forward and hopefully improve the quality of their lives despite the trauma, tragedy, and uncertainty of their return to singlehood."

> Maurice Rappaport, M.D. Ph.D.
> President, Northern California
> Psychiatrist Assn.

"This work fills a real need, not only for those who have lost a loved one, but for their friends who often feel helpless in their efforts to comfort and help them."

> Kenneth Cambon, M.D.
> Professor Emeritus
> University of British Columbia

SUDDENLY SINGLE!
A Lifeline For Anyone
Who Has Lost a Love

Hal Larson & Susan Larson

HALO BOOKS
San Francisco, California

Published by:

HALO BOOKS
Post Office Box 2529
San Francisco, CA 94126

Manufactured in the United States of America

Library of Congress Catalog Card Number
89-15348

Library of Congress Cataloging-in-Publication Data

Larson, Hal, 1924-
Suddenly Single!

   Includes index.
    1. Grief. 2. Bereavement – Psychological aspects.
3. Loss (Psychology) 4. Separation (Psychology)
5. Death – Psychological aspects. 6. Single people –
Psychology. I. Larson, Susan, 1952-   . II. Title.
BF575.G7L37 1990   155.9'37   89-15348
ISBN 0-9622874-6-6

for Iola

ACKNOWLEDGEMENTS

The authors are deeply indebted to the groups and individuals in the U.S., Canada and Mexico whose experience and insights are the very fiber of this work.

Without their candor, generosity, patience and encouragement, the book would never have been written.

Particular thanks go to Dean Salama, M.D., M.R.C.P., Ridgewood, New Jersey; Jane A. Bouma-Saldana, Marital and Family Therapist, Mexico City; Kenneth Cambon, M.D., Professor Emeritus, University of British Columbia; Gary Harbaugh, Ph.D., Trinity Lutheran Seminary, Columbus, Ohio; Mariano Barragan, M.D., Founder of the Mexican Institute of Psychotherapy; Dr. Maurice Rappaport, President, Northern California Psychiatric Assn.; Marc I. Ehrlich, Ph.D., Marital and Family Therapist, Mexico City; Roderic Gorney, M.D., Ph.D., U.C.L.A., Raymond Morrow, Ph.D., U. of Alberta, Canada; Jerrilu Johnson, A.A.M.F.T, Family Psychologist, Mexico City; John A. Buehler, M.D., Ph.D., Kentfield, CA; Carolina H. de Kiewek, Mexico City; H. Samm Coombs, Lagunitas, CA.; Barbara V. Stroud, Shelton, WN.; Capt. I. A.H. MacTavish, Victoria, B.C.; Bruce Decker, former Chairman, California AIDS Advisory Commission; Ralph Holmstad, Sausalito, CA.; Russ Coughlin, San Francisco, CA.; Richard Rojas, Novato, CA.; Barbara Cox, Mill Valley, CA.; Mitchell Forster, Esq., San Francisco, CA.; Paula Bard, San Francisco, CA; Daisy Araica, San Francisco, CA.; Richard McLean, Mill Valley, CA. Jack de Celle, Fairfax, CA.

While the authors sought the counsel of many of the finest psychiatrists and therapists in the U.S., Canada and Mexico, what appears on these pages is the responsibility of the authors alone.

Similarly, while highly respected professionals were consulted, and every effort made to assure that material herein is as sound and helpful as possible, the authors do not represent that this work is an alternative to professional help. "Suddenly Single!" is intended as a general background and guide, and the authors and Halo Books shall have neither liability nor responsibility for any alleged damage resulting from the information and advice herein. The purpose of the book is to provide what help it can to people in need of help.

Cover by Susan Larson

[vi]

TABLE OF CONTENTS

[I]

THE BEGINNING

Chapter One. SUDDENLY!
Your Love Is Gone and Your World Is Upside Down

Chapter Two. THE ANATOMY OF GRIEF
What You Need To Know Immediately

[II]

THE MIDDLE

Chapter Three. EMOTIONAL SHOCK
Part I. What Is Happening?

Chapter Four. EMOTIONAL SHOCK
Part II. What Can You Do About It?

[vii]

Chapter Nine. WITHDRAWAL
Part II. What Is Happening?

We slide into self-pity. 🌿 We feel unattractive. 🌿 We avoid friends. 🌿 We fear rejection. 🌿 We are often tired. 🌿 Memories are exaggerated. 🌿 Our resistance is low. 🌿 We wear a mask. 🌿 We become depressed. 🌿 Depression impedes healing. 🌿 It can signal danger. 🌿 Anger burns down.

Chapter Ten. WITHDRAWAL
Part II. What Can You Do About It?

Like yourself again. 🌿 Learn to relax. 🌿 Get rid of tension. 🌿 Ask for help. 🌿 Accept being alone. 🌿 Don't get impatient. 🌿 Plan your holidays. 🌿 Don't hide your grief. 🌿 Keep supportive friends. 🌿 Strengthen religious ties. 🌿 Stop punishing yourself. 🌿 Unload old baggage. 🌿 Make small changes. 🌿 Review your progress. 🌿 Begin to let go. 🌿 Speak for yourself. 🌿 Speak for your love. 🌿 Leave nothing out. 🌿 Say good bye. 🌿 Think about it. 🌿 Make new friends. 🌿 Suicide is no answer. 🌿 Consider the alternatives.

Chapter Eleven. HEALING
Part I. What Is Happening?

We are coming back. 🌿 Single is different. 🌿 Some things never change. 🌿 We have learned. 🌿 Life has new meaning.

Chapter Twelve. HEALING
Part II. What Can You Do About It?

Widen your world. 🌿 Brighten your world. 🌿 Challenge yourself. 🌿 Do things for you. 🌿 Set attainable goals. 🌿 Discover the good in people. 🌿 Love yourself.

[III]
THE ENDING
Chapter Thirteen. SINGLE!
What Have We Learned?

We are stronger. ❧ We are more alive. ❧ We have survived. ❧ Love is always new. ❧ It is up to us. ❧ We have choices. ❧ We give love.

PREFACE

This book was written because it didn't exist.

A dear friend lost her husband of many years. The authors looked everywhere for the right book to help her through a terrifying time.

The book they sought would explain in layman's language what was happening to her.

It would tell her what she could do to ease the trauma of her loss.

It would be something she could read in a few hours, something she could return to when she needed help.

It would not be a course in applied psychology, and it would not be feel-good fluff.

The authors could not find the book, so they wrote it.

They wanted the book to be a genuine help to people desperately in need of help.

Anyone who has lost a love should find help here, whether the loss is from divorce, separation or death. Each is a form of death, and all are painful.

It is the earnest hope of the authors that you will find in this book a light to help you find your way through this most difficult time.

ABOUT THE AUTHORS

Both authors know first-hand the loss of a love.

HAL LARSON has written, lectured and taught for three decades. He did his undergraduate work in Oregon and graduate studies in Massachusetts. His first wife died after a lengthy illness.

SUSAN LARSON earned both graduate and undergraduate degrees in California. Her first marriage ended in divorce after eight years. The couple divide their time between San Francisco and their home in Mexico.

[I]
THE BEGINNING

The soul would have no rainbows
had the eyes no tears.
　　　　　— John Vance Cheney

> Life is like an onion; you peel it off
> One layer at a time, and sometimes you weep.
> — Carl Sandburg

Chapter One
SUDDENLY!

your love is gone, and your world is upside down.

You have suffered a crushing loss.

You hurt all over.

And you don't know what is happening to you.

All you know is that you ache

because you have lost your love.

> *The joys of love are but a moment long.*
> *The pain of love endures your whole life long.*
> — *Jean Martini*

Help is here.

This book will help you live through your loss.

It will help you understand the scary things
that are happening to you now.

The tears, the fears, the panic in the night.
The numbness, the pain, the utter, utter loneliness.

The guilt, the self-doubt, the trembling hands.
The chilling conviction that no one understands.

This book will explain those things and more
and suggest how you can best cope with them.

This book is about loss and grief and healing.
And emerging strong and confident and whole.

And it's about love.

Because there can be no grief without love.

> *Is it, in heav'n, a crime to love too well?*
> — *Alexander Pope*

Grief is the cost of love.

Grief is what happens
when a whole love becomes halved.

It is the inevitable cost of loving.

Grief is mourning that part of ourselves
that we gladly gave
and lost, together with our love.

This book is your guide
through grief and into healing.

We are not alone.

It helps to know we are not alone.

Everyone, at one time or another,

in one way or another,

suffers the loss of a love.

Mother, father, sibling, husband, wife, lover, child.

Most of us suffer loss more than once.

And no one is ever prepared for it.

> *Give, oh give me back my heart.*
> — *Lord Byron*

We are never ready.

Even if we have seen it coming for a long time,

we are not ready when it happens.

We may think we can prepare ourselves,

but we are never ready.

Movies end when lovers get together.

That's not the way it is in real life.

In real life, getting together is a beginning.

That's when the story starts.

It's the beginning of a journey together.

Love is the beginning.

> *O'er thee the sun doth pine*
> *And angels mourn.*
> — *Robert Bridges*

The real adventure of life

begins when we love.

And in real life there is pain

when we lose our love.

The books we read didn't prepare us for that.

The movies we saw didn't prepare us for that.

Nothing prepared us for the loss of a love.

Nothing we have seen or done or learned
has made us ready for this.

Nothing.

> *Once I laughed when I heard you saying*
> *I'd be playing solitaire,*
> *Uneasy in my easy chair.*
> *It never entered my mind.*
> — *Lorenz Hart*

The pain will go away.

Good friends and this book
will help us through the hurt.

But the pain is something we must experience.
And we must do that alone.

The pain will go away.
only to return again,
and go away for a longer time.

And our life will shape itself

around those comings and goings,

like cypress roots clinging to granite boulders.

But the loss will always be there.

And we must learn to accept that loss

> *But two are walking apart for ever,*
> *And wave their hands for a mute farewell.*
> — Jean Ingelow

Endings become beginnings.

Life is made of endings and beginnings.

First light signals the end of night

and the beginning of a brand new day.

Winter ends and Spring begins.

Spring gives way to Summer,

which segues into the beginning of Autumn.

[7]

The endings become beginnings.

In truth, the ending creates the beginning.

That is the cycle of life.

> *And the seasons, they go round and round.*
> *And the painted ponies go up and down.*
> *We're captive on the carousel of time.*
> *—Joni Mitchell*

Loss can strengthen us.

Like iron that is tempered with fire,

we can become stronger through our loss.

It is difficult for us to see that now.

And it certainly is not the path we would chose.

But if we do the work of grieving

as outlined in this book,

we will acquire a new tensile strength.

We will be stronger, more sure of ourself,

ready to move ahead with the rest of our life.

Well, Everyone can master a grief but he that has it.
— William Shakespeare

Chapter Two
THE ANATOMY OF GRIEF
What You Need To Know Immediately

Right now, your mind is fighting your body.

You have taken a crushing blow.

The greatest emotional stress you can endure

comes from the loss of a love.

You are under very severe pressure.

But part of your mind

is saying business as usual.

It is telling you that you should not feel the loss.

> *From perfect grief there need not be*
> *Wisdom or even memory.*
> — *Dante Rossetti*

Let yourself feel.

You have been taught from childhood
to bottle up your feelings.

You have been told
that feeling and showing grief
are signs of weakness.

Society says that grownups
should never show their hurt.

But it's not society that is hurting.
It's *you.*

Accept your loss.

The single most important thing you can do now
is accept your loss.

Let yourself feel all the emotion of your loss.
Give yourself permission to grieve.

Allow yourself to feel and express
what your body is telling you.

Trying to control your feelings does not help.
Trying to be "strong" gets in the way of healing.

When you accept and feel your loss,
you will be starting the long road back.

> *Bone of my bone thou art, and from thy state*
> *Mine shall never be parted.*
> — *John Milton*

Grief is not weakness.

Feeling your grief is not a sign of weakness.
It is an essential part of healing.

What you are feeling is normal and necessary.

Those feelings will stay with you
until you allow them out.

Let yourself feel them and talk about them.
Open the bottle and let them out.

Don't be "brave".

Well-meaning friends may say "be brave"
or "you'll feel fine tomorrow."

That kind of advice
invalidates your feelings,
trivializes your loss.

Don't be brave.

You will not feel fine tomorrow.
You will still hurt something awful.

And you will hurt a whole lot longer
if you try to deny your feelings.

> *I bid farewell to every fear,*
> *and wipe my weeping eyes.*
> — *Isaac Watts*

Do your grieving.

True friends allow you to grieve.
They help by giving you permission
to feel and express your loss.

You are grieving for more than your love.
You are grieving for the death of a future
and for a part of you that is gone forever.

You are grieving for the death of a dream.

You are grieving for the end

of what you were together.

And for the wholeness that became halved.

> *And I scarce know which part may greater be,–*
> *What I keep of you, or you rob from me*
> *— George Santayana*

Don't deny your feelings.

What you need to do is begin the work of grieving.

You need to work through your pain.

Accept it. Feel it. Talk about it.

You are finding that you can't control your feelings.
So you may become distrustful of them
and then try to deny them.

You can't make those feelings go away
by not talking about them.

They will still be there,
struggling to get out.

The hurt lingers longer
when your feelings are denied.

> *Parting is all we know of heaven,*
> *And all we need of hell.*
> — *Emily Dickinson*

Loss is part of life.

Think about this:
The only way you can live without loss
is to live without love.

You have opened yourself to love.

And now that love is gone.

You have suffered a terrible loss.

And it hurts like hell.

It is going to continue to hurt

until you have completed the grieving process.

> *Say what you will, 'tis better to be left*
> *than never to have been loved.*
> *— William Congreve*

Grief is not sickness.

Considering how long grief has been around,

not much is known about it.

And most of what is "known" is incorrect.

You have heard people say
that someone is sick with grief.

But grief is not a sickness.
It is a necessary part of healing.

It is as normal as laughter.
And tears.

Grief is a process.

Grief varies considerably between people,
in both intensity and duration.

The intensity tends to vary with
how much of yourself you invested in your mate.

The duration varies principally with
your willingness to go through the process.

Grief *is* a process.
It does not hold still.
You feel differently about it every day.

Grief wears many faces.

Grief is yin and yang.

It is both laughter and sadness,
heightened activity and inactivity,
anger and relief.

It is never the same.

In fact, the very sets of opposing emotions
illustrate the uniqueness of grief.

Grief has no schedule.
It will do what it will do.

> *Ah, woe is me! Winter is come and gone,*
> *But grief returns with the revolving year.*
> *— Percy Bysshe Shelley*

You must help.

Time does not heal all wounds.
You have to participate in the healing.

But if you open yourself
to the grieving process,
the hurt will begin to leave.

Therapists used to believe
that grief travels through predictable stages –
from despair to acceptance.

They thought that if your grief did not
follow that precise pattern,
you were not "normal".

> The grief that does not speak
> Whispers the o'er-fraught heart, and bids it break.
> — William Shakespeare

There is no "normal".

It is now known that
grief has no pattern.

It is not neat and orderly and linear.
And there is no "normal".

Every person is different,
so every grief is different.

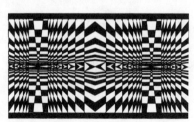

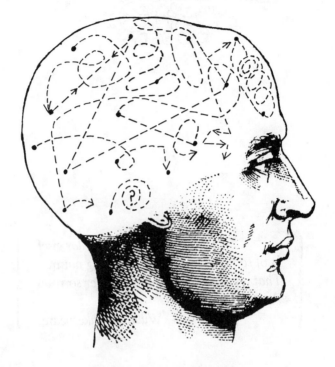

The essence of grief is fundamental,
but your experience with it is unique.

The elements of grief may appear in any order.

Grief may begin with anger
and bounce into shock and denial
and back again to anger and guilt.

The path of grief cannot be predicted.

> My particular grief
> Is of so flood-gate and o'erbearing nature
> That it engluts and swallows other sorrows
> And it is still itself.
> — William Shakespeare

[II]
THE MIDDLE

This main section of the book explores the elements of grief.

Each element will be looked at in two ways:

First, a chapter about what is happening to you.

Then a chapter dealing with how you can best cope with it.

You may wish to skim the book and return later to areas of concern to you.

Or you may prefer to read the whole book leisurely.

[26]

> *If a man will begin with certainties, he shall end in doubts; but if he will be content to begin with doubts, he shall end in certainties.*
> — *Francis Bacon*

Chapter Three
EMOTIONAL SHOCK
Part I. What Is Happening?

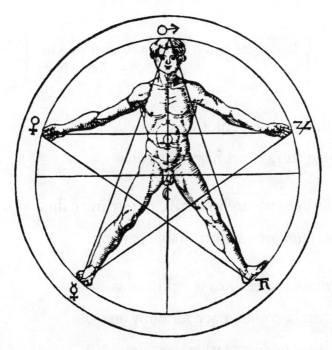

We may go into emotional shock

when we learn of our loss.

Shock is both bad news and good news.

It can take us into extreme anxiety,
which can produce troubling erratic reactions.

It can also protect us.

We may become unpredictable.

> *But, O the heavy change, now thou art gone.*
> — *John Milton*

While we are in emotional shock,
strange things can happen to us.

Sometimes we are in a still, unsettling calm,
sometimes an uncontrollable panic.

Normal connections may elude us.
We can become unaccountably anxious
and display dissociative reactions.

We are capable of utterly irrational behavior:
things we would normally never do.

And we probably won't remember them later.

Clarity comes and goes.

Sometimes when we are in emotional shock,
periods of utter clarity take over.

Then they disappear without a memory.

We may emerge briefly from shock
and experience anger, sadness, loneliness,
or a host of tangled emotions.

Grief has no pattern.
It travels where it must.

Shock also insulates us.

Electric eels, I might add, do it,
though it shocks 'em, I know.
  — Cole Porter

When we sustain a physical injury,

shock protects us from pain

until we are better able to handle it.

The same kind of thing happens

when we experience severe emotional stress.

[30]

Our nerves become numb.

We are shielded from reality.

Our circuits won't accept more information.

We are insulated

from the intensity of our emotions.

Habit takes over.

> *My heart aches, and a drowsy numbness pains my sense.*
> —*John Keats*

We are functioning on autopilot.

Habit is taking over.

Later, friends may tell us

that we functioned calmly and efficiently.

"No one would know you had a problem," they say.

"You were managing everything."

But it is not really us.

It is the autopilot at work.

[31]

Chapter Four
EMOTIONAL SHOCK
Part II. What Can You Do About It?

There is not a lot you can do right now.

The autopilot switch is on.

The important thing now
is not to demand too much of yourself.

Avoid trying to do too much too soon.

Permit good friends to help.

Avoid more stress.

Your body is protecting you.

Return the favor by doing things for it.

Begin a modest exercise program.

Try to eat sensibly; take vitamins.

Give your body extra sleep and rest.

Avoid activities that add to your stress.

You have about all you can manage.

Avoid using tranquilizers, sleeping pills,

narcotics or excessive alcohol.

Your system is getting natural anesthesia.

These substances "distance" you from your feelings,

deprive you of true experience,

lengthen your trip back.

In truth, you would do well to avoid drugs

and alcohol throughout the grieving process.

> *I tell you, hopeless grief is passionless.*
> — *Elizabeth Barrett Browning*

Give yourself time.

You will frequently get the feeling

that you must make important decisions fast.

Don't.

There will be time for that later.

Those decisions can wait.

And you are not thinking clearly now.

Do not rush into major decisions.

Give yourself time.

> *Life may change, but it may fly not;*
> *Hope may vanish, but can die not.*
> — *Percy Bysshe Shelley*

> A deep distress has humanized my soul.
> — William Wordsworth

Chapter Five
PROTECTING YOUR EGO
Part I. What Is Happening?

A pivotal part of our cultural conditioning
is a belief in the permanence of things.

"I'll always live here in this house."

"Mom and Dad will always be here."

"My love and I will always be together."

We wrap these beliefs around us like a security blanket.

We want to believe things will stay the way they are.

It is simply more comfortable that way.

> Since 'tis Nature's law to change,
> Constancy alone is strange.
> — John Wilmot

Loss denies permanence.

When we lose our love,

our belief in permanence is challenged.

Loss contradicts one of our most basic beliefs.

It tells us that things we know

simply may not be so.

This gives our internal computer

a very large headache.

It creates doubts

about our whole belief system.

"If *this* is not true," we ask ourself,

"what other 'truths' may be found wanting?"

We reinvent the truth.

> *Hope is a good breakfast, but it is a bad supper,*
> — *Francis Bacon*

Rather than accept the possibility

that our basic beliefs are wrong,

we try to make facts conform to those beliefs.

We reinvent the truth.

We may deny or refuse to hear anything

that reinforces the painful truth of our loss.

We may even destroy things that deny our reality.

We try to change the world outside our head
because it hurts too much
to change the world inside our head.

Loss threatens our ego.

Our sense of ourselves, our ego,
is structured within our belief system.

In fact, our fiction of the permanence of life
is a product of our ego.

And when loss challenges that belief,
it becomes a serious threat to our ego.

Damage to our ego is something we do not want.
So we activate a battery of devices to protect it.

These ingenious defense devices
are selected by our unconscious mind
to keep our ego out of harm's way.

Consciously we have little hand in it.

What we *can* do, however,
is influence how long we need those devices
by our willingness to go through the grieving process.

> *I have lived long enough, having seen one thing,*
> *that love hath an end.*
> — *Algernon Swinburne*

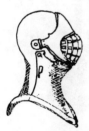  

We activate defense devices.

To defuse the threat to our ego,
our unconscious mind selects
from a large arsenal of defense devices.

The suddenness of our loss
is a major determinant
in that selection.

The more abrupt the loss,
the greater the need
for our ego to protect us from harm.

What defense devices do
is lift emotions from one circumstance
and move them to a place they don't belong.

They generally provide short-term relief
and long-term mischief.

> *Like the dew on the mountain,*
> *Like the foam on the river,*
> *Like the bubble on the fountain,*
> *Thou art gone, and for ever!*
> *— Sir Walter Scott*

Repression.

Repression is the king of defense devices
that go to work when we suffer loss.

When we repress,
we reject responses we don't like
and send them to free-float in our unconscious.

We repress when the idea is too painful
or the impulse too frightening.

Our feelings about our loss may be so intense
that we simply can't cope with them.
So we repress our feelings.

[43]

> *All the rivers run into the sea, yet the sea is not full.*
> — *Ecclesiastes*

Repression often serves a short-term purpose:
we don't have to deal with our feelings now.

But the feelings are still there,
and they must be dealt with some time.

The feelings we repress will eventually come out.
They may emerge when we least expect them.
But come out they will.

Repression can become a habit,
a way of denying all our feelings.

It can cost us our capacity to feel.
And not to feel is not to be alive.

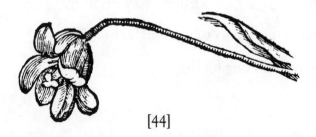

Denial

> For if it be but half denied,
> 'Tis half as good as justified.
> — Samuel Butler

Denial is refusing to accept an unpleasant fact.
We all use it — generally as a delaying tactic.

We deny the truth until our ego
is healthy enough to handle it.

"Not me," we say. "This can't happen to me."

"It can't possibly be so.
My mate is just gone for a while."

Denial is often harmless,

but when we cling too long to our fictions,

we are letting problems accumulate.

And the longer we deny,

the more we delay healing.

> *And wilt thou leave me thus?*
> *Say nay, say nay, for shame!*
> *— Sir Thomas Wyatt*

Bargaining

We bargain with ourselves — or God —

to change or postpone the inevitable.

"Let it not be true,

and I'll be a better person."

"Bring back my love,

and I'll devote my life to good causes."

(We probably won't keep the promises.)

[46]

Like most defense devices,

bargaining serves a delaying function.

It helps us buy time until our ego is ready.

It also delays the healing process.

> *For present joys are more to flesh and blood*
> *Than a dull prospect of a distant good.*
> — *John Dryden*

Projection

Projection is a way to get rid of unacceptable anger.
We simply move it to someone or something else.

If we are angry with our mate for leaving,
we may take it out on the kids
because we can't accept being angry with our love.

If we loathe ourself for failure in business,
we may redirect our anger to our boss
because self-contempt is too hard to deal with.

Projection is blaming others
for what we see in them
but cannot see or accept in ourself.

Projection is scapegoating.

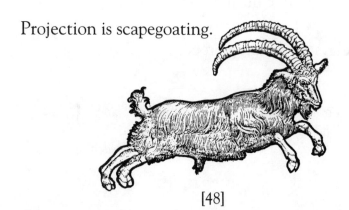

One of the pitfalls of this defense

is that at some level we understand that

we are defending against the consequences of loss.

This keeps the loss itself in the forefront.

And it becomes a formidable barrier to healing.

The ultimate form of projection is paranoia,

which makes everyone and everything else the problem.

In my beginning is my end.
— *George Eliot*

[49]

> *Neurosis is always a substitute for legitimate suffering.*
> — *Carl Jung*

Chapter Six
PROTECTING YOUR EGO
Part II. *What Can You Do About It?*

What you need to do now
is engage in some healthy introspection.

Which of the defense devices is serving you?
Which is impeding the healing process?

How long have you been relying on them?
Is it time to let go and begin facing your loss?

This is the worst of times
to be dishonest with yourself.

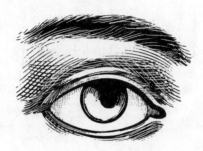

The more you accept the truth now,
the shorter your road back.

Rebuild your self-worth.

You may be building little road blocks
to hinder your journey to recovery.

Are you continuing to hide things
that remind you of your mate?

Are you clinging to your pain
because you think it will help you
"bond" with your lost love?

Are you refusing to talk about your loss?
Are you avoiding friends you used to see together?

> *Silence augmenteth grief.*
> — *Baron Brooke*

Now is the time to clean up your act.

Remove those barriers to healing.

Rebuild your sense of self-worth.

Be aware that
your ego may try to hinder your efforts
to build back your self-worth.

Listen to your ego but don't trust it.

Hear it and let it be.

The better you feel about yourself,
the less you will need defense devices.

Like yourself more.

Do things that help you like yourself.

Exercise your mind and body.

Give yourself small challenges.

See people you like to be with.

If they don't invite you, invite them.

You may find that doctors want to sedate you
or give you pills to help you sleep.

That may sound appealing when you hurt.

But try to avoid being drugged.

Drugs mask your feelings, close off grief.

And you must experience your grief.

> *And grief itself be mortal!*
> — *Percy Bysshe Shelley*

[54]

Watch your diet.

Try to avoid both under- and over- eating.

If you have trouble eating,
think of food you craved as a child:
cornflakes, hot dogs, popcorn, whatever.

If your problem is unprecedented over-eating,
you are probably trying to eat your troubles away.

In reality, of course,
you are eating your way
into a whole new problem.

Without knowing it, you may be building
an extra layer of fat
to protect you from reality.

It won't work.

Give yourself an ultimatum:

over-eating must stop *now!*

If you continue serious over-eating,

get professional help.

Help others.

> *Teach me to feel another's woe.*
> — *Alexander Pope*

The best way to help yourself

is to help others.

Think of your friends in need of help.

Get involved in community or group projects.

When you are doing things for others
your own problems tend to diminish.

There is simply no better way
to take your mind off your problems
than to help others in need.

You may find others
going through similar experiences.
You can help each other.

> *Can I see another's woe,*
> *And not be in sorrow too?*
> *Can I see another's grief,*
> *And not seek for kind relief?*
> *— William Blake*

Begin a diary.

Now is a good time

to begin a notebook or diary.

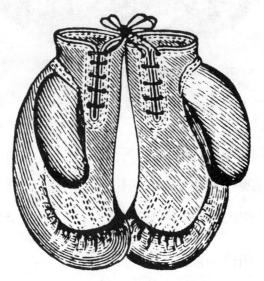

Record the day and write down what you feel.

Don't pull your punches.

Be honest with yourself.

> *If they asked me, I could write a book,*
> *About the way you walk and whisper and look.*
> *— Lorenz Hart*

Write down *feelings*, not events.

Also try to record your dreams

and how you feel about them.

Don't worry about grammar or construction.

You are writing for your eyes only.

It is important that you do not edit these thoughts.

Write them as they occur to you.

Sit down right now and write what you are feeling.

And then read what you wrote.

Try to do this every day.

You can monitor your own healing progress.

> The weight of this time we must obey,
> Speak what we feel; not what we ought to say.
> — William Shakespeare

[59]

> *Anger is a short madness.*
> — Horace

Chapter Seven
ANGER & GUILT
Part I. What Is Happening?

When we emerge from shock,

we feel the pain.

And we get angry.

With friends, ourself, God, our love.

Everyone.

We are mad at everyone.

We get angry with our friends because

they have not lost their mates and they don't hurt.

We get angry with ourself because we feel that somehow we are responsible for our loss.

We get angry with God because our loss is unjust.

We get angry with our love because
it is not fair to leave us with so much to do.

We get angry because we are frustrated
and don't know how to release the pressure.

We bottle up our anger.

> *Not to be sad she tries,*
> *Still — it's lonely lies.*
> *— Walter de la Mare*

We learn as children to censor our feelings.
We learn that nice people don't get angry.

We are taught, in short, not to feel.

And because we learned we should not feel anger,
we bottled it up inside.

Or we redirected it to our unconscious mind.

In either case, it is still there,
waiting to come out and create more problems.

Denied or repressed anger can turn into
intense bitterness or self-pity,
both debilitating consequences.

It can also lead to depression,
which is anger turned inward.

> *O love! Thow bane of the most generous souls!*
> *Thou doubtful pleasure, and thou certain pain.*
> — *George Lansdowne*

We must learn to feel.

Our throwaway society complicates the problem.

From childhood we are taught
that anything can be replaced.

Toys, pets, clothes:
all were part of a throwaway world.

"Don't cry," we were told.
"We'll get you another."

If we did not learn how to feel loss as a child,
we will likely have trouble with it as an adult.

Farewell! thou art too dear for my possessing.
— William Shakespeare

[64]

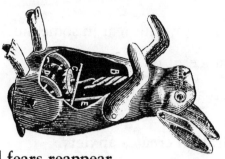

Childhood fears reappear.

In a child's closet of terror
lurk two particularly vexing fears
which can re-emerge to complicate adult loss.

One childhood goblin is Fear of Abandonment.

A mother was hurrying
along a crowed city street.

Running after her, crying uncontrollably,
was a five-year old on the edge of panic.

"Go away. I don't want you any more.
You've been bad," shouted the mother.

Experiences like that can leave indelible impressions.

Most children know this fear in some measure.

In some instances it is outright terror.

And it is then as terror that it resurfaces.

Fear of separation creates anxiety.

> *Absence from whom we love is worse than death.*
> — *William Cowper*

The other childhood fear that can be released

from our unconscious mind by an adult loss

is Separation Anxiety.

Many of us have nightmares as children

about losing our parents –

particularly our mother.

Losing our love can trigger this childhood anxiety,

perhaps nestled in the unconscious for decades.

It resurfaces to intensify the emotions of our loss

and create a panic we can't comprehend.

Upon examination, the terror will likely abate.

If not, we should seek professional help.

The ego is damaged.

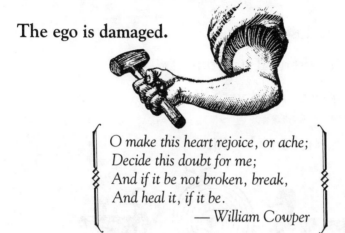

> *O make this heart rejoice, or ache;*
> *Decide this doubt for me;*
> *And if it be not broken, break,*
> *And heal it, if it be.*
> — *William Cowper*

Notwithstanding the armada of defense devices,

the ego will inevitably take some punishment.

Loss has diminished us.

Our relationship with our mate

is generally the core of our life.

It determines, in very large measure,

how we define ourself.

It shapes us: who we are,
what we feel, how we behave.

So when we lose our love,
we lose the essential structure
that has given meaning to life.

Our ego has taken a big hit.

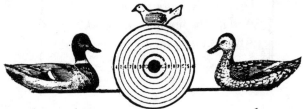

There is, happily, an upside to ego punishment.
As the ego is damaged, the self emerges.
And the self is stronger and more unifying.

Moreover, the grieving process
allows us to become less egotistical
and become more truly who we are.

But we cannot see that yet.
Our loss overwhelms us.

What Is Happening

We lash out.

The very framework of our life is damaged.

And in our hurt and frustration, we strike back.

At anything and everything.

Not only is our principal support system shattered;

our underlying beliefs have been sundered.

We have been seared by incendiary truths:

That everything is not replaceable.

That we are not going to be together forever.

That things are not okay, after all.

That we have been reduced to half a whole.

That the future is not at all what we thought.

That we are suddenly, utterly alone.

[69]

We experience mood swings.

We are sailing in uncharted waters.

Our old maps tell us nothing.

Our comfortable routine is gone.

Our basis for self definition has been crushed.

Our belief system is splintered.

Everything is different.

We experience wide mood swings.

We are on an emotional roller-coaster.

With all that support gone,

anger rushes in to fill the vacuum.

Change makes us angry.

> *To be interested in the changing seasons is a*
> *happier state of mind than to be hopelessly in*
> *love with spring.*
> — George Santayana

Anger seems to come from every point on the compass.

Much of it comes from frustration with ourself.

We have lost control of the situation.

Things are happening without our direction.

A major source of our anger is change itself.
Change is a threat.

Most of us are more inflexible than we realize.

The inflexibility that is so obvious in others
we can rarely recognize in ourself.

Few things are more threatening
than the breaking of long-time habits.

In fact, we may miss the comfortable routine
almost as much as we miss our love.

Even if the routine was uncomfortable,
we miss and are threatened by its loss.

We feel guilty.

Because we feel we have lost control of our life,
we become increasingly frustrated and angry.

We become upset with ourself for being angry.

Then we feel guilty about that.

We become angry with our mate

for not being there.

But we know we are being unfair.

So again we immerse ourself in guilt.

We love and hate at the same time.

Then we feel guilty for hating.

> *So sweet love seemed that April morn,*
> *When first we kissed beside the thorn,*
> *So strangely sweet, it was not strange*
> *We thought that love could never change.*
> — *Robert Bridges*

Guilt is self-inflicted pain.

We blame ourself for our loss:

We must have done something to cause it.

Or we failed to do something to prevent it.

Guilt is tortured anger: self-inflicted pain.

We acquire the knack for it early in life.

Guilt is something we learn as children.

"If you are bad, God will punish you."

Or Daddy or Mama or Santa or the Devil.

We carry that into adulthood.

"My love is gone because I was bad."

> *My stronger guilt defeats my strong intent.*
> — *William Shakespeare*

We transfer childhood guilt.

We may be carrying old childhood guilt —

perhaps from the death of a parent.

When we introduce this unresolved guilt
into an adult situation like the loss of our love,
we are engaging in transference.

Transferring childhood guilt
can greatly exacerbate the problem of adult loss.

If we feel intense guilt about our loss,
we should examine it for transference.

It may belong to a different time.

Current guilt is enough.

> *Sorrow breeds sorrow, one grief brings forth twain.*
> — *Michael Drayton*

Transferring childhood guilt
impedes the healing process.
It can induce destructive behavior.

We should always question and challenge our guilt.

Nonetheless, a certain amount of guilt is inevitable.

We are trained from childhood to accept responsibility.

And because events require explanations,

we conclude that we were somehow responsible.

We proclaim ourselves guilty.

Guilt is a choice.

Guilt can be a singularly disabling emotion.

It can take us to the edges of hell.

It can be a formidable barrier to healing.

Its roots are often buried deep in our unconscious.

It comes from the need to explain:
someone or something must be at fault.

Guilt is, nonetheless, a choice we make,
and it is usually based on flawed assumptions.

The more we examine it, the weaker it becomes.

Guilt is frequently the most painful part of loss.
When we unload it, we become curiously energized.
The most hurtful part of loss is behind us.

> *I mourn'd, and yet shall mourn with ever-returning spring.*
> — *Walt Whitman*

> *Those thing that hurt, instruct.*
> — *Benjamin Franklin*

Chapter Eight
ANGER & GUILT
Part II. What Can You Do About It?

One continuing theme of this book
is that you must let the anger come out.
Do not deny it or repress it.

Recognize that releasing your anger
is essential to the grieving process.

There are a host of ways you can do this.

Get the anger out.

> *Nothing ever becomes real till it is experienced.*
> — *John Keats*

Go ahead and kick the sofa, punch the pillow.

Hop up and down, shout, stomp, throw things.

Yell "I'm really mad about this!"

Do whatever you feel like doing —

as long as it is not hurtful to you or others.

Also, use your anger energy constructively.

Paint a picture, plant a garden, help a friend.

Use the energy constructively.

Think of other positive uses

for your anger energy.

Redecorate. Do Spring cleaning, whatever the season.

Find constructive ways to get the anger out.

It may wear you out, but it is a good tiredness.

You are keeping a daily diary now.

Tell it about your anger and guilt.

Write down everything you are feeling.

> I remember the way we parted,
> The day and the way we met.
> — Algernon Swinbourne

Write, draw or talk.

If you are not keeping a diary

because you are uncomfortable about writing,

draw pictures of what you are feeling.

Remember: it does not have to be lasting art;

you are doing it to express your feelings —

and to get your anger out.

If you have trouble with writing and drawing,

express your feelings to a tape recorder.

Just talk; do not edit your feelings.

Say everything you are feeling.

Then wind it back and listen to what you said.

Separate the parts.

> *We carry within us the wonders we seek without us.*
> — *Sir Thomas Browne*

Sit down and examine your anger.

The best way to do that is to separate the parts.

When all the pieces to your jigsaw puzzle

are jumbled together in a box,

it makes no sense at all.

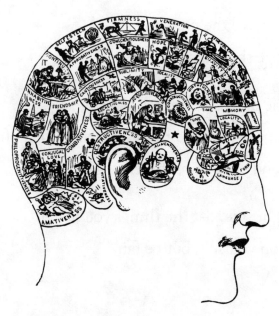

But when you examine them one by one,

you can put them in their proper place

and watch the complete picture emerge.

What was confusion becomes clear.

Balance it out.

> Pure and complete sorrow is impossible as pure
> and complete joy.
> — Leo Tolstoy

When you have the parts separated,

do a balance sheet of yourself.

Draw a line down the center of a page.

On the left side, list the things you are proud of:

family, friends, accomplishments, good deeds.

On the right side, list the things you regret.

Be tough on yourself, but be fair.

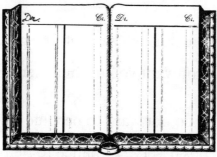

Study the two columns for a while.

You will probably find you are not so bad, after all.

You likely have far less reason to dislike yourself
than you thought you had.

> *Life is a hereditary disease.*
> *— Graffito*

Let friends help.

Do not spend too much time alone.

Let good friends know you want to see them.

You are probably not as bad company as you think.

When you are with your friends, level with them.

Let them know how you are really feeling.

They realize you must go through the process.

And they do not want you to shut them out.

Of course, you do not want to become a pest.

But good friends deserve a chance to help.

> *Friendship doubleth joys, and cutteth grief in halves.*
> — *Francis Bacon*

Eliminate "bad air".

Do deep breathing exercises.

Pump out the "bad air".

(That is what your body does when you hyperventilate.)

Continue your exercise program.

You need to burn up a lot of anger energy.

This is a good time to meditate.

If you have never done it, give it a try.

Put your mind and body at rest.

> *A good cure for insomnia is to get plenty of sleep.*
> — *W.C. Fields*

Release anger safely.

Let your anger come out when you are alone
or with good friends or support groups.

But do not release anger when you are driving,
at work, in a public place, or around harmful objects.

And do not do it when you are angry with yourself.

You may become attached to your anger.

But that is just a way to avoid looking inside yourself.

And looking inside is generally more painful
than staying with your anger.

It is harder and more painful
and vastly more helpful.

Look inside yourself.
Let go of your anger.

Talk it out.

Have a conversation with yourself.
Talk about how you are really feeling.
Tell yourself all the things that are making you mad.

Talk about the guilt you are feeling.
Discuss how unnecessary that guilt really is.

Make fun of your guilt.
Tell yourself how dumb it is.
Expose your guilt for what it is.

Nobody can be responsible for everything.
Not even you.

Imagine yourself wrapping up your guilt
and burying it in the garden.
Burying it forever.

Examine your guilt.

> *I'll be this abject thing no more;*
> *Love, give me back my heart again.*
> — George Lansdowne

Here is a quick test for needless guilt:

Are you deliberately making yourself hurt
over something you had no control over?

Let that monkey go.

Are you punishing yourself now
because of some unresolved long-ago guilt?

Set yourself free.

You have taken another step
on the road back.

> *A feeling of sadness and longing*
> *That is not akin to pain,*
> *And resembles sorrow only*
> *As the mist resembles rain.*
> — Henry Wadsworth Longfellow

Chapter Nine
WITHDRAWAL
Part I. What Is Happening?

Anger is an exhausting emotion.

So we are worn out when the anger is spent.

It is not uncommon now to withdraw into ourself.

We feel lonely, empty, deserted.

Our energy level is very low.

We are likely to feel victimized, betrayed.

We slide into self-pity.

The unpredictable mood swings return.

We feel bitterness, resentment, self-pity.

[91]

These feelings come over us like a cloud
and then they blow away
only to return with the next breeze.

We are frequently disoriented, out of phase.
Our feelings are both intense and irrational.

Part of the reason for our disorientation
is a sense that we have become incomplete.

We had been part of something larger than ourself.
We defined ourself by that unity.
Now it is gone, and we are undefined, tentative.

In sooth I know not why I am so sad.
— William Shakespeare

We feel unattractive.

We have never been so alone.
We are missing part of ourself.

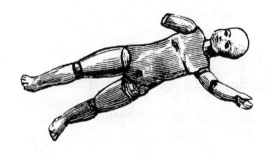

We may even have nightmares
about losing an arm or leg.

No matter how irrational,
these fears are very real to us.

Our childhood fear of abandonment may reappear.
And that provokes another bout of self-doubt.

If our mate abandoned us,
we must be undeserving, undesirable,
unattractive, unimportant.

We avoid friends.

> In that sweet mood when pleasant thoughts
> Bring sad thoughts to the mind.
> — William Wordsworth

Because we feel so negative about ourself,

we may withdraw from social contacts.

We think we make friends uncomfortable.

When we are around friends,

we tend to keep them off-balance.

We invite them to talk about our loss.
But when they touch a nerve, we shut them out.

They may avoid discussing our loss
because they do not want to see us hurt.

Or because they are also feeling
more vulnerable to change and pain.

Then we conclude that they don't care,
so we become angry with them.

We fear rejection.

When we shut out our friends,
we are acting out of emotional hurt:
we are afraid of being rejected again.

We are not ready yet to risk being hurt.

Sometimes we need to be alone.
But loneliness, too, can be hurtful.

[95]

Alone, we listen for familiar sounds.

The silence of loneliness can be crushing.

Our mind plays tricks on us.

We are certain we see or hear our mate.

At the door. In the shower. In a crowd.

> *What happiness? Who can enjoy alone,*
> *Or all enjoying, what contentment find?*
> *— John Milton*

We are often tired.

During withdrawal, our mouth is likely to become dry,
our throat and jaw muscles tense.

We have trouble concentrating.

We lose our appetite — and likely some weight.

We seem to be tired most of the time.

We sigh a lot and have trouble sleeping.

We may have sudden and unpredictable crying fits.

Seas of melancholy sweep over us.

[96]

Memories are exaggerated.

> *There's in you all that we believe of heav'n,*
> *Amazing brightness, purity, and truth*
> *Eternal joy, and everlasting love.*
> — *Thomas Otway*

When we think of our lost love,

memories tend to become exaggerated.

Our mate was kinder, meaner, sweeter, tougher.

The good times were better, the bad times worse.

Sometimes we retreat into fantasies.

We are sure our mate is coming back.

We are convinced we are missing a limb.

We are, of course,
missing part of ourself.

We are missing the part of ourself
that we gladly gave to our love.

We gave it in joy and wonder
and grieve it in pain and sorrow.

> And love's the noblest frailty of the mind.
> — John Dryden

Our resistance is low.

Our vision is narrow now;
we are seeing through pain.

Because our resistance is low,
our body is particularly vulnerable,
a candidate for every vagrant virus.

In brief flashes of startling clarity,

we recognize that we are deceiving ourself,

that we live in an unreal world of our own making.

We swing emotionally from pole to pole.

One minute we are victim.

The next minute, a very special person.

> *The rose's scent is bitterness*
> *to him that loved the rose.*
> *— Francis Thompson*

We wear a mask.

We feel a lot of plain old-fashioned sadness.

That, too, is a necessary part of the grief process.

Denying our loss burdens our body.

It can result in tension, headaches, even ulcers.

In some measure, we all try to deny our loss.

We find ever-more ingenious ways to deceive ourselves.

We wear a mask to conceal our hurt.

From others and from ourself.

And then we forget
which is the mask
and which is us.

Wearing the mask saps our energy.

And it contributes nothing.

Our energy to live comes from within us,

not in maintaining the mask.

> *A stage where every man must play a part,*
> *And mine a sad one.*
> — William Shakespeare

We become depressed.

During withdrawal we are likely
to tumble into depression.

It is a troubled time.
Depression can be scary.
Sometimes it is a black, bottomless void.

Among its symptoms are insomnia, appetite changes,
weakness, drowsiness, headaches and heavy perspiration.

Depression is anger turned inward.
It interrupts the grieving process.
It plays havoc with our stabilizing gyroscope.

Depression impedes healing.

Depression blocks our grieving channels
and frustrates the process of relieving our anger.

Yet it seems to be necessary to grieving.
It weaves in and out throughout the process.

The first frightening wave often sweeps over us
when we first fully comprehend our loss.

It is intense, frightening and often painful.
But it is unlikely to last very long.

Depression often comes from fear of the future,
fear that something terrible could happen.

The fear is almost always unfounded, irrational.

> *Methinks nobody should be sad but I.*
> — *William Shakespeare*

It can signal danger.

Depression now can signal destructive behavior.

When it appears during withdrawal,
thoughts of suicide can intrude.
This is a time to seek help.

The next chapter outlines
steps to be taken.

Anger burns down.

Incongruously, the onset of depression
can also be a sign of hope.

It is the severest form of anger,
the white heat that flares at the end.

When depression occurs during withdrawal,
it likely means anger is beginning to burn out.

It is the beginning of the end of hurt.
We are starting to let go.

> *With all my will but much against my heart,*
> *We two now part.*
> — Coventry Patmore

> This is not the end. It is not even the beginning of
> the end. But it is, perhaps, the end of the beginning.
> — Winston Churchill

Chapter Ten
WITHDRAWAL
Part II. What Can You Do About It?

Focus on getting your act together.

Make a lot of lists:

Lists of things you should do now.

Lists of things you can delay until later.

Lists of books to read, people to call.

Lists of letters to write, shows to see.

Lists of those projects you have been putting off.

Assign yourself tasks.

And reward yourself when you do them.

Make a point of trying something new every week.

> *Growth is the only evidence of life.*
> *— Cardinal Newman*

Like yourself again.

Do things that help you like yourself.

Go to concerts and the theater.

Read those books on your to-read list.

Have a long talk with family members.

Get out of the house and spend time with friends.

Bring discipline to your eating habits.

Eat a healthy, balanced diet.

Keep your head clear.

Continue to steer clear of pills, drugs, alcohol.

Be sure you get the sleep you need.

But find ways to avoid staying in bed too long.

For example, have friends make wake-up calls.

> *When so many are lonely as seem to be lonely,*
> *it would be inexcusably selfish to be lonely alone.*
> *— Tennessee Williams*

Learn to relax.

Exercise your mind: read, study, solve problems.

Exercise your body: walk, run, do exercises.

Practice yoga. Meditate. Learn to relax.

Here is one easy technique to help you relax:

Sit comfortably with both feet on the floor.

Close your eyes and think of your favorite color.

Now inhale slowly, filling your lungs.

Hold for five seconds, concentrating on your color.

Then exhale slowly, completely, and hold three seconds.

Repeat the process two more times.

Keep concentrating on your color.

Now open your eyes and you will find

your whole body is relaxed.

> *Those things that are requisite and necessary,*
> *as well for the body as the soul.*
> *— The Book of Common Prayer*

Get rid of tension.

Another good procedure to help you relax:
Tense every muscle in your body.

Begin with your face muscles
and work your way down to your toes.

Hold for a count of ten and relax all at once.
The tension is gone.

Experiment with variations of these exercises.
You will find the two or three that work best.

Ask for help.

Don't be afraid to ask for help.
Tell a friend you really need to talk.
A good friend will understand.

But do not clam up when your friend arrives.
Be sure you are ready to discuss everything openly.

Call your friend when you are in a good mood,
not when you are feeling desperate.

That way you will have an open line
when you are desperate for help.

Accept being alone.

Try to come to terms with being alone.
You don't cure it; you accept it.

But do not let yourself wallow in loneliness.

The best way to handle being alone
is to learn to be comfortable with yourself.

If you put a little effort into it,
you will likely find you are very good company.

Being alone is not necessarily being lonely.

> *Farewell, farewell, the heart that lives alone.*
> — *William Wordsworth*

Don't get impatient.

Things are starting to come together now.
You may be getting anxious to move on.

That is a healthy signal.

But you are probably still not ready
to make those major decisions you have postponed.

Now is not the time to sell the house
or move to another city or take a cruise
or move in with your relatives.

There is more grieving work yet.

[113]

Plan your holidays.

Anniversaries and holidays are tough.

Plan ahead for those difficult days.
Be with family or friends. Help others.

Plan a full schedule for those days.
They will still hurt.
But not as much.

On those remembered days
do not try to protect others from your sadness;
do not try to tough it out alone.

> *Our sweetest songs are those that tell of saddest thought.*
> — *Percy Bysshe Shelley*

Don't hide your grief.

There is no reason to be ashamed of your grief.
Don't try to hide it from others.

And if there are children,
don't be afraid to let them see you grieve.

That gives them permission to let it out, too.

Do not work at forgetting;
the memories are there.

And don't try to rush the process.
Grief will not be hurried.

Permit yourself to forgive two people:
your love and yourself.

> *All the sadness in the sweet,*
> *The sweetness in the sad.*
> *— Francis Thompson*

Keep supportive friends.

Your ego is still fragile, easily bruised.
Thoughtless or cruel "friends" can damage it.

Supportive, understanding friends
smooth your way through the grieving process.

But "friends" who diminish your self-worth
are not the friends you want around you.

Let those people know the harm they are causing.
In most instances, they will change their ways.

If they continue to impede your healing,
you will be better off not seeing them.

Strengthen religious ties.

If you are a member of an organized religion,
this is a good time to reaffirm those ties.

Spiritual support can help ease your burden
and provide healing peace of mind.

> *Blessed are they that mourn: for they*
> *shall be comforted.*
> — St. Matthew

A note of caution is indicated here:

Religions tend toward rigid views of morality,

and they can rekindle all the old guilt.

The support you receive can be a great blessing.

But do not accept any guilt trips.

Your ego does not need that now.

[117]

Stop punishing yourself.

Another potential source of ego damage
is someone you must continue to live with:
You.

Ask yourself some hard questions.

Have you built road blocks on your road back?
Are you punishing yourself with inappropriate guilt?
Are you actively looking for faults in yourself?

Write down the ways you are injuring your ego,
the ways you are not allowing yourself to develop.

Now slowly draw a line through each.
And promise yourself to stop doing it.

You have enough to do without fighting yourself.

> *No blessed leisure for love or hope,*
> *But only time for grief.*
> — *Thomas Hood*

Unload old baggage.

Walk up the stairs to your mental attic.
Look around for old baggage.

Open up your old suitcase of hurts.
Examine the ancient wounds carefully.

They are recorded on old calendars.
The guilt, the fears, the hurt belong to another time.

You will travel lighter on the road back
without that ancient, unnecessary baggage.

Make small changes.

It is time now to consider making minor changes:
in your habits, attitude, behavior.

Think about positive changes you would like to make.

Do you want to be more outgoing?

More relaxed? More giving? More fun?

If you think you have been too reclusive,

venture out more socially.

If you still feel tense,

work on the relaxation exercises.

If you have been intellectually dormant,

look for ways to stretch your mind.

> *A timely utterance gave that thought relief,*
> *And I again am strong.*
> — William Wordsworth

Review your progress.

After a week or so, examine the results.

Are the changes in the right direction?

Do they make you happier, more at peace?

If they do, venture a little farther.

Experiment with some more significant changes.

Now review the results of those changes.

Are you continuing to move in the right direction?

Continue experimenting and expanding.

You are becoming steadily stronger, more confident.

Begin to let go.

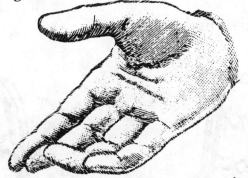

> *Love is a circle that doth restless move*
> *In the same sweet eternity of love.*
> — Robert Herrick

You come now to the hardest task of all:

Letting go of your lost love.

Of the dozens of different approaches to this,
most successful over time is the gestalt method.

It takes a bit of effort and some courage.
And if you enter into it honestly, it works.

Do this when you are alone and your head is clear:

Place two straight-back chairs facing each other.
Imagine your mate sitting in one.
Now you sit in the other.

Speak for yourself.

Now talk about what has been on your mind.
Tell your love how you really feel.

Be honest: get your true feelings out.
And say everything on your mind.

Talk about the shock, the guilt, the loneliness.
Talk about the unfairness of having to cope alone.
Talk about your anger, your frustration, your hurt.

Talk about your love.
Cry. Laugh.
Remember.

> *Most musical of mourners, weep again!*
> — *Percy Bysshe Shelley*

Speak for your love.

When you have said everything you have to say,
get up and sit in the other chair.

Now you are your mate talking to you.
How would your love answer what you said?

Some of it would likely be critical.
Some of it would be angry.
Some of it sad.

When thou art absent I am sad.
— Caroline Norton

Some of it would be kind and loving.
Some filled with the music of remembered laughter.

And there would be questions.

Leave nothing out.

Say all those things your love would say.

Ask all of the hard questions.

Do not hold back, even if it hurts.

Be fair to your mate.

Leave nothing out.

> *If thou must love me, let it be for naught*
> *Except for love's sake only.*
> — *Elizabeth Barrett Browning*

Have you said everything, answered everything?

If you are sure you have,

get up and sit again in your original chair.

Say good bye.

Now think carefully about what your love said.
And respond fully to all questions and comments.

Bring up things you forgot the first time.
Say everything you have on your mind.
Everything.

And then say good bye.

You have just made a giant step on the road back.

> *Our everlasting farewell take:*
> *for ever, and for ever.*
>   — *William Shakespeare*

Think about it.

Reflect now on the remarkable conversation
you just had with your love.

What did you learn?

Almost certainly, there were some surprises,
some wisdom that had been eluding you.

Think, too, about what you just did:
You said good bye to your mate.

You let go.

> *I see that all things come to an end.*
> — Book of Common Prayer

Make new friends.

You will begin noticing something different now.
You. You have changed considerably.

You have gone through a great deal.
Your perspective has changed.

This could be a good time to meet new friends.

You will, of course, keep your real friends.
But some acquaintances are no longer around.
Your ordeal revealed which are your true friends.

New friends likely share your new interests.
They broaden your world, expand your horizon.

Let these new friendships develop naturally.

Suicide is no answer.

Before leaving this chapter on withdrawal,
it is necessary to discuss the question of suicide.

It is during this time of grieving
that thoughts of suicide may occur.

If they do, here are some things you should consider:

You are in a time of personal crisis.
Your judgement is not at its best.

If you are trying to send a message to someone,
talk to that person.

That way, you will be around
to hear the response.

Consider the alternatives.

If you are trying to punish someone,
examine why you are.

And is suicide better than talking about it?
Talk it over with a good friend or religious advisor.

Suicide may be a question.
But it is not an answer.

Remember: you can still change your mind.

> There has to be something, somewhere, something, somewhere,
> Somewhere, something that you like.
> — Martin Charnin

If you are still contemplating suicide,

dial your operator immediately

and ask for the Suicide Hot Line.

Do it *now*!

Chapter Eleven
HEALING
Part I. What Is Happening?

We know we are on the way back

when we can remember without pain,

when we wake up refreshed and happy.

We know it when

we look ahead more than back,

when we can look back without the too-familiar pain.

We will still hurt.

But it is not the old intense, malignant hurt.

This hurt is more comfortable, even nostalgic.

The energy has gone out of it.

We know we are coming back
when our jokes no longer have an edge,
when we can see loss as part of life's cycle.

We are coming back.

We know it when
we think and dream of something else,
when we feel physically and mentally alive.

We know it when someone says
we have not talked about our loss for hours,
when we start thinking of new clothes.

> *The summer days and summer ways,*
> *How bright with hope and bliss.*
> — *Robert Service*

We know it when
we notice how vivid the colors have become,
when we feel a new rush of energy.

We know it when a remembered song or sound
is no longer a piercing thorn,
but a sweet reminder of what was good.

We know it when we get excited about
something we didn't know of yesterday.

We know it when we can finally say good bye.

Single is different.

Many of us never learned how to be single.

We came together at an early age
and shaped our values and beliefs together.

> *No, there's nothing half so sweet in life*
> *As love's young dream.*
> *— Thomas Moore*

[133]

We formed our friendships as a couple,

developed our daily routines as a couple,

formed our view of the world together.

Everything changed when we became suddenly single.

It is a whole different life.

Our needs are much the same as they were,

but the world around us is very different.

Some things never change.

We keep the sweet parts of our past.

Our *basic* values and interests are unchanged.

And our true friends are still with us.

Some things will never change.

But now we also find new doors to open.

We do things we have never done before:

things we had no idea we could do.

We have become more secure with ourself;

we are better able to cope with the world.

[134]

> I mourn for that most lovely thing; and yet
> God's will be done.
> — William Butler Yeats

We have learned.

Traveling through grief has taught us a great deal.

We have learned how very precious love is.
We have learned the wonder of true friendship.
We have learned to look at life in a different light.

We have learned that a whole lot of things
we thought were important
aren't.

We have learned there is more to life
than "serving" another.

We have learned that our own life
is the only one we can live.

We have learned that growth is problem-solving,
that problem-solving is frequently painful.

[135]

We have learned that life is the business of
trading solved problems for unsolved problems.

> *I've looked at life from both sides now.*
> — *Joni Mitchell*

Life has new meaning.

Life is different now.

It has taken on a richer texture.

It is at once painful and wonderful.

We no longer look for our love

in a crowd or coming up the walkway.

Our energy and self-esteem are higher.

We sense we are nearing our goal.

Now we can come out from behind our mask.

Now we are able to face our loss.

*By trying we can easily learn to endure
adversity. Another man's, I mean.*
— *Mark Twain*

Chapter Twelve
HEALING
Part II. What Can You Do About It?

From here on, it is mostly downhill and shady.

But don't try to sprint the rest of the way.

Healing has its own rhythm.

The important thing to do now

is work through any remaining anger.

When anger no longer dominates your life,

you can see it more clearly.

Widen your world.

Work at broadening your horizon.

Examine the world around you.

Smell the roses.

Explore new things to do:

new activities, schools, groups, trips.

Re-examine your old habits and routines.

Are they right for the person you have become?

If not, let them go.

> *So sad, so fresh, the days that are no more.*
> — *Alfred, Lord Tennyson*

Brighten your world.

Take a look at your immediate environment.

Could it stand a bit of brightening?

What better time to start than now?

Paint the walls.

Paper the halls.

Put some color in your life.

Consider a new wardrobe.

Plant some flowers.

Color your life happy.

Brighten the world you live in.

Challenge yourself.

Stretch.

Grow.

Challenge yourself more.

And *now* is a good time to start considering

those major decisions you have been postponing.

What Can You Do About It?

Maybe you really should

sell the house, take a cruise,

move to another city, change careers.

Maybe.

Now you are ready to handle those choices.

Take your time. Think it through.

Then do what you decide is best.

Do things for you.

One of the nicest things you can do for yourself

is to nurture your new friendships

and help them blossom.

But don't try to force them into old molds.

Let them find their own level.

[143]

Think of other things to do for yourself.

A little pampering is in order now.

A massage. An elegant dinner. A resort weekend.

Do something for yourself every day for a week.

Keep a record of it in your diary.

There is nothing wrong with being good to yourself.

Give yourself time and space

to change and to grow.

> *Nor love thy life, nor hate; but what thou liv'st*
> *Live well, how long or short permit to Heaven.*
> — *John Milton*

Set attainable goals.

You do want to challenge yourself now.
But you do not want to over-reach.

Set goals for yourself.
But set reasonably attainable goals.

If you do not reach one of your goals,
do not count it a failure.

"Failure" is a frame of mind, not a reality.
It is an essential part of the pattern of life,
a way we make decisions for the future.

Consider the things you want to do with your life.
Things *you* want to do: not what others expect.

And then design a game plan for doing them.

Discover the good in people.

This is a time of discovery and rediscovery.

Discover again the good in yourself and others.

Learn how to be at peace with yourself again.

> *Live thou thy life beneath the masking sun*
> *Till Beauty, Truth, and Love in thee are one.*
> — *Robert Bridges*

Rediscover your sense of humor.

Learn to laugh again.

Do not dedicate your life
to not being hurt again.

There will inevitably be other hurts.
That is part of the contract of living.
But now you are better able to cope.

And if you ever again lose a love,
it will be a different kind of loss,
because of the change and growth in you.

Now you understand that loss

goes with the territory —

and life goes on.

Enjoy.

Love yourself.

Help others.

It is the best way to help yourself.

Savor all the joys of being single and whole.

Rejoice in your growth.

Learn to believe in yourself again.

Learn to love yourself again.

Loving yourself is a beginning.

For more than gold was in a ring, and love was not a little thing
Between the trees in Ivywood, when all the world was young.
— G.K. Chesterton

> To every thing there is a season, and a time
> to every purpose under heaven
> — *Ecclesiastes*

[III]
THE ENDING

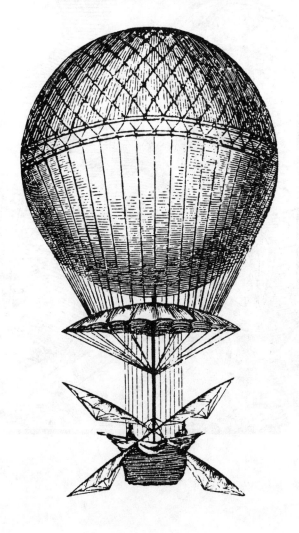

> *Throughout the whole of life*
> *one must continue to learn to live.*
> — *Seneca*

Chapter Thirteen
SINGLE!
What Have We Learned?

We have learned that permanence is an illusion
and that the illusion can cause great mischief.

It obscures the inevitability of loss.

Nothing in life is forever.
Not life itself.

Our time with our mate is finite.
It has a beginning and an ending.
That is part of the rhythm of life.

We have let go of the illusion of permanence.
And we have accepted the pain of our loss.

> O, love's but a dance,
>   Where Time plays the fiddle!
>   — Henry Dobson

We are stronger.

We have accepted the pain of loss.

And we have become tempered by the process.

Because we have done the work of grieving,

we are strong and healthy and complete.

We have been severely tested

by the searing pain of loss,

and we have emerged whole.

There will be other surprises, other losses.

But there will also be joy and wonder.

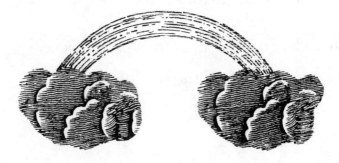

We are more alive.

> *With an eye made quiet by the power*
> *Of harmony, and the deep power of joy,*
> *We see into the life of things.*
> — William Wordsworth

The experience has made our life richer.

We know what a precious gift life is.

We have learned to treasure each day
as though it is the last day.

We will never promise ourself never to love again.
That is simply a way to avoid being hurt again.

And it could cost us a chance
for a whole new wholeness.

[153]

We have survived.

We know that we must trust again,
let ourself be vulnerable again.

We know that the old pain ends,
but the loss will always be there.

We know that we have survived:
we are still here.

> *Heaviness may endure for a night, but joy*
> *cometh in the morning.*
> — *The Book of Common Prayer*

Love is always new.

We know there is more to come
and that it is time to get on with our life.

We know we can be hurt only if we expect too much—
from others or from ourself.

We know that any relationship
is limited and imperfect.

We know we can never prepare to love,
because every person and every love is unique.

We know we always love for the first time.

It is up to us.

We know that we can truly belong
to only one person:
ourself.

We know we are responsible for our own life.

We know that holidays and anniversaries
will always be difficult.

We will remember,
and we are okay.

> *Joy is the sweet voice, joy the luminous cloud –*
> *We in ourselves rejoice!*
> *— Samuel Taylor Coleridge*

We have choices.

We are secure enough to enjoy single life.

We are open enough to love again.

We are free enough,

strong enough,

to be ourself.

The past was a nice place to visit.

But it is not a good place to live.

Now a door is opened.

And streaming through the doorway

is the bright sunshine of the future.

> *I dipt into the future, far as human eye could see,*
> *Saw the vision of the world, and all the wonders that would be.*
> *— Alfred, Lord Tennyson*

[157]

We give love.

We know that we need
to keep reinventing ourself.

We know that we don't find love:
we *give* it.

We know that we never really owned our mate.
Our love was loaned to us.

We know that we have a life,
and we are going to live it.

We know that this is now, today.
It is a good place to live,
and we are glad we're here.

> *Glittering like the morning star, full of*
> *life, and splendor and joy.*
> — *Edmund Burke*

INDEX

YOUR COMMENTS ARE WELCOME

The authors and Halo Books invite
your comments, criticism and suggestions.

Write to Halo Books, Box 2529,
San Francisco, CA 94126.

If you wish to order
additional copies of "Suddenly Single!"
please send your name and address together with
$12.95 for each book
plus $1 shipping for one book
and 50¢ for each additional book.
In California please add 6% sales tax.